APPALACHIAN NEWGROUND

By

Lee Pennington

Lee Pennington

APPALACHIAN NEWGROUND

Published by Winchester Cottage Print

In Louisville, KY

Printed by LSI, Nashville, TN

U.S.A.

Cover and design by Jill Baker

Illustrated by Jill Baker

First Edition

Printed in the United States of America

Copyright 2016

DEDICATION

FOR JILL, ARTIST EXTRAORDINAIRE

Lee Pennington

APPALACHIAN NEWGROUND

TABLE OF CONTENTS

LIST OF ILLUSTRATIONS
BY JILL BAKER

ACKNOWLEDGEMENTS

THE AUTHOR WISHES TO THANK THE FOLLOWING PUBLICATIONS WHERE CERTAIN MATERIAL IN APPALACHIAN NEWGROUND FIRST APPEARED:

GREEN RIVER REVIEW, WRITERS NOTES & QUOTES, ADENA, BLUEGRASS REVIEW, GREENUP NEWS, THE SPIRIT OF '76, UNITED POET, PENNINGTON PEDIGREES, PEGASUS, POEMS & PRINTS, CUMBERLANDS, AMERICAN POET, ALTOONA MIRROR, THE ANGELS, THE GUILD, THERE COMES A TIME, POET (INDIA), DOWN INK LANE, SEED, CONTEMPORARY KENTUCKY POETRY, PROMISING POETS OF THE MIDWEST, EXPERIMENT, SOUTHERN POETRY REVIEW, BAY SHORE BREEZE, APPALACHIAN SOUTH, ASPECTS, MIDNIGHT, SEYDEL QUARTERLY, AMANUENSIS, JEAN'S JOURNAL, BOARDER, LOUISVILLE GAZETTE, MOUNTAIN REVIEW, RED CLAY READER, POEMS FROM THE HILLS, POETRY PREVUE, SELECTED KENTUCKY LITERATURE, CARAVEL, AND FIDDLEHEAD.

BOOKS BY LEE PENNINGTON

The Dark Hills of Jesse Stuart (criticism), 1967
Scenes from a Southern Road (poetry), 1969
Poems and Prints (poetry), 1969
Wildflower Poems for Joy (poetry), 1970
April Poems (poetry), 1971
Appalachia, My Sorrow (drama), 1971
Songs of Blood Harlan (poetry), 1975
Spring of Violets (poetry), 1976
Coalmine (drama), 1976
The Porch (drama), 1976
The Spirit of Poor Fork (drama), 1976
I Knew a Woman (poetry), 1977
Ragweed (drama), 1980
The Janus Collection (poetry/photography), 1982
Foxwind (drama), 1984
Appalachian Quartet (drama), 1984
The Scotian Women (drama), 1984
Thigmotropism (poetry), 1993
Appalachian Newground (poetry), 2016

Appalachian Newground

Lee Pennington

PERSPECTIVE

You have called me the land;
have said my eyes' roots
go down in ancient dirt.

Then swirl I
trying to be unafraid to love
bony ridges dying men
rusting plows crying women-
children hung across their hips,
bones themselves like ridges.

And if I am the land,
the place where I hear weeping,
and who, if not I, is there left
for my brother's keeping?

And, yes, for what it's worth,
If I am me
I am the earth.

Lee Pennington

INTRODUCTION, FOREWORD, OR SOMETHING

Appalachia is a broken mirror and as such, a place of many contrasts—a land of mystery and obvious, a land of song and sorrow, a land of warmth and chill, a land of living and dying, a land of high mountains and deep valleys, a land of people brilliant and people unknowing, a land of hope and hopelessness, a land of richness and worthless, a land of truth and lies, a land of motion and standing still. It is a land America once forgot and now one she's forgetting to remember.

One cannot hear the name without turning aside, pausing, wondering, for there is hardly a person alive who has not in some way been touched by this land and these people. Appalachia has literally fed all the great cities with bodies her own-any land's greatest gift, her people—and now even these, generations removed, return sometimes in spirit to search for what was lost in the passing, what perhaps never was anyway except in false memory.

Many colored quilts cover the searchers, guitars and banjos bathe songs in music remembered, and deep in the trees a stillness hangs—this beyond the screaming pain of noisy crowds and the familiar wail of sirens.

Even so, even to want to know is to realize loneliness is the hearse we ride in. To retrieve such music, coverings, and all else, is an attempt to grasp the forgotten of perhaps what never was, is no more than holding a tiny piece of the broken mirror where we see only half a face, our own, and then realize the seven years have just begun.

Appalachia's people, although mostly British Isles stock, came from everywhere and went likewise. They came to this land of promise, themselves giving promises—they both the gift and the giver. Inherent in it all they lived by nourishment of the land and likewise nourished it in dying.

They cleared the land, plowed and planted and grew first crops abundant. Later they stripped the timber and even later dug the coal. With each new season the land grew old and often burdened beyond hope, eventually died silently. Now many old fields turn back to timber where leaves go down make the ground, what's left of it, again new.

Whatever she is, wherever she touches, Appalachia symbolizes America's dream, and even if we wake in nightmare she is the night we all must sleep through and morning come must go our waking way beyond the dreaming.

Within Appalachia's myth is a metaphor for us all. We must ask and wonder where she's been, where she is, and where she is going. We must answer with fire whether it warm us or burn us.

I am Appalachia's son, born of her, raised of her to manhood. I am also a stranger to her. Still I search in her for the dream, our dream, the American dream—hidden somewhere, I believe, between the clearing and the fields now trees again. Perhaps hidden is not the right word. Perhaps a better world be lost—now and forever. Or maybe even never was.

I hold in my hand pieces of the broken mirror, myself part of the glass. This then is my attempt, however futile, to put some of it, if only one piece, back together.

Lee Pennington

Appalachian Newground

WHERE DO SHADOWS GO?

Lee Pennington

Where do Shadows Go? (Eagles)   *by Jill Baker*

Lee Pennington

WHERE DO SHADOWS GO?

It was so long ago I can hardly remember. Way back there in the dusty corners of memory is where it is, and I am looking on the spider web valleys with the sun falling to the tune of wind. It is back beside dawn when the birds carry the morning shadows away and leave only singing. It is back beside the rough hillsides now soft in memory and beside the white floating clouds and the quick rains eating up the dusty roads and leaving glassy leaves in the eyes.

And what do I remember? I remember the sled load of farm tools drawn on a road of rocks and ruts and the scrape of wood on stone is in my mind. I remember the fields, out from the wooded earth, and the winding rows filled with spindly corn in battle with the weeds. And the swinging hoes splintering stumps and stones and raising dust and the talk above the sounds of times and men.

We farmed then only thirty-two acres and all this, except for less than a half-acre squeezed in the valley, was bound to the sides of many small, rough mountains. There was, too, above it all the ridge land and this was the land my father loved, for it was land on which he could stand and know the sky, and he loved the land and sky. Above it all there was a roughness in his voice which found gentleness in the wind, like the end of thunder in the soft clouds. His was not a race with time, though he lived by the sun, but a communion with the land and sky. He talked to the land and it answered. He talked to the wind and the sky and there was return. Others standing around him often heard nothing but he was speaking and they were answering—he, his land, and his sky.

Then it was a rough battle. There were eleven brothers and sisters and the land. My father, my mother, my brothers and sisters and I fought the newground in the winter, cleared away the trees and stumps for spring plowing, piled brush for spring burning, with the stinging snow in our faces, with the warm wood stoves of the evenings in our minds. We thought it hard and spoke often of the hardness but never once let the axes know of our pain. No tears fell to rust the shiny blades.

We were with it at dawn and with it at dusk, and all in between and the night came around to rest us.

My father was first to rise, always before the sun or even before the shadows began to slip away and hide under the trees. Then my mother who greeted each morning like a smiling violet. Then they called our names and we each crawled from the covers and put on shirts, pants, and shoes and dipped the icy rain water from the barrels and splashed our faces with excitement. Around the breakfast table, always full with eggs, bacon, biscuits, jelly, milk, coffee, there was a quietness and my father's big voice gave thanks, not for money, for we seldom had very much of that, but for another time and another meal. We ate heartily and quickly. And often, most often, before the sun and still with dew, the fields knew our weight and heard our easy talk and sounds of plows and hoe. Fresh, cool dirt fell from the plow, sometimes my father's and sometimes mine, and dust like swarming bees flew from the hoes. This was spring when the maples blushed red and sassafras were pale green. This was the early rains falling and the tiny mountain streams gathering mud to carry away to the sea. Spring was the budding trees and the odors of the early blooms and working shirt free to feel the sun—a time to plant and gamble against a late frost, and my father standing in late evening on the ridge against the sky, watching the sky, watching the red fingers touch the tree tops or the blue ridges swallow the sun. The sky was red, tomorrow would bring rain; the sky was clear, tomorrow no falling weather.

My father knew the sky and land and told us, as we worked together in the fields, what to expect and not to be disappointed if it did or did not come. He planted early tomatoes in the coves where the river fog made a warm blanket against the death grey frost. He planted corn to catch the evening dew and drip dampness into the spider leg roots to fight dry times, and he planted with the evening sky red so tomorrow's rain would excite the winter dried seeds.

But we were in the newground where the tiny yellow locust roots refused to die, where stumps tried for three seasons to become trees again. This land we cleared last winter, my father, my mother, my brothers and sisters and I. We cleared with the snow in our faces. We burned the brush and the grey-white ashes had long since succumbed to the plow and parts had blown on the wind. Now the tender, yet hardy, green sprouts tried to return, and at times I felt my father was sad for having taken over where all once was green. He took only what was needed and never a tree fell on land that would not be farmed. Still he was sad. Often I've seen him take a coffee sack full of pine cones off to a bare spot in the timberline and plant them and now the trees are tall and have shadows of their own and their roots know the earth and their needles know the sun.

Weeds and sprouts lay in the soft morning shadow of the mountains, weeds our hoes had torn from the earth, and they lay green and fresh till the morning sun rose over the tree tops and found them there and left them suddenly crisp and dry. The fresh, dark earth, turned from the plow, also met with the sun and the color of the soil changed to a light tan. As the day wore on, clean slashes edged around the hill and rows of tiny, pale corn stood like blushing children. My father plowed and we followed with our gooseneck hoes, followed till the day was gone and we stood leaning on our hoes with the mules biting grass by the road and my father watching the sky. Tomorrow it would rain.

Summers were hot with sweaty leaves and the squirrels barking love notes to each other while we picked purple raspberries to paint our fingers and tongues, while we began to gather in what my father told us would come. Tomatoes hang red in my memory beside the shredded blue overall coat hanging faded on a cross of a scarecrow, and still the slick black crows caw, cawing in the wind. High in a dead oak sat the watcher who spoke to a field of other crows and the blowing wind on the scarecrow only made him fluff his wings and caw, caw again. But my father did not mind for he loved the crows and shared with them his harvest, left corn standing in the late autumn fields so crows and others on the wing could find something to eat when the white snows filled the valleys, the hillsides and the ridge tops near the sky.

We were alone in the summers—my mother, my brothers, my sisters and I. Each day my father drove away with a truck load of things we had raised—corn, beans, tomatoes, berries, potatoes, beets—drove to the hot city streets where he called out the names of what he had and they came, those hiding from the hot sun, and bought vegetables grown on the land near the sky. But we were alone gathering what summer had ripened and planting what late autumn would know, planting late corn and October beans.

Autumn found us there. We pulled up the multicolored October beans and carried them to a shade tree and sat on baskets turned upside down and drank fresh, clear water to cool our thirst. All day we worked till the baskets were full and we took those from under us, and sat on stones, and filled the remaining empty baskets. We loaded the stripped beans on the sled and took them to the valley below and met my father home from a long day of streets and sun and we loaded his truck for another day.

And this was autumn with the giant poplars sending their yellow eagles on the wind and the red maples and sassafras and sumac following and the land covered with a blanket of many colors, and the smell of late autumn apples around the sound of yellow jackets working on those already fallen, and the sound of jarflies constantly ringing in the day and the katydids whispering of frost in the night. Squirrels barked at each other and played in the tall hickory trees of the ridge. We gathered in the last of the harvest—pumpkins like bright yellow-orange eyes constantly looking, the corn in tent fodder shocks except that left for the crows, the sweet potatoes from their long narrow mounds on the ridge. This was going to the woods with our baskets and gathering hickory nuts, hazel nuts, walnuts and some acorns to roast on the open winter fire.

The leaves fell till the trees stood bare and their black arms reached a final gesture toward the sky. We took blankets, we in pairs so there was a hand for each corner, and we filled them with the newly fallen leaves and we carried these to the empty fields and left them in great piles, left them for the wind to spread. My father wanted always to leave the field better than he found it and the leaves would do that by returning rich black top soil to the earth. The wind played with the leaves till the whole field knew their movement. They danced to unwritten music and finally settled there and became part of the land.

Winter came again and we were waiting with our axes sharpened and the tall foreboding mountains asleep with the dark dead trees. I turned the grey wheel, the soft whetting stone, and my father held the axes and star eyes fell off of the edge. We dipped the blades in water and steam rose the color of the wheel into the crisp, thin air.

This time we would go to the north side where the winter snows laid silent and white long after the south side was melted. Here we would plant peach trees where the snows would hold back the early blooming and save the fruit from the late spring frost. But first there was the clearing, the cutting of the dark trees and their black arms swishing toward the earth, the cutting and trimming and piling up the brush for burning, piling around the stumps now sticking up their heads in frightful agony. It was a sad time for my father. I watched him many times fondle a tree and look off into the valley, look at the winter sky, and look back again at the tree before the sawing. He measured the new acre with his eyes and seldom missed by more than a few feet and no trees beyond his imaginary line ever fell.

Before the burning we worked a path of fresh earth around the whole piece of newground and later walked the path to see that no branch had fallen over and that no leaves had blown a bridge across for the fire to travel. We all took our places around the new land and each one set to burning the area in front of him. The fires, thirteen of them, crawled slowly toward the middle, catching along the way the waiting brush and with it the sounds of screaming green timber and exploding rocks flying into a million tiny pieces. The flames reached high and colored the sky red, but this was our doing, and tomorrow it would not rain. Soon the flames were down except for the many red-orange eyes where the brush piles had been and we gathered and chunked each one and the flames rose again.

In the spring after the plowing, after the cutter plow had torn loose roots and dug out stones, we went along and planted two seeds in each place we wanted a tree. Later, when they had sprouted and broken through the dark earth and sent out shoots and bore young, tender leaves, we returned and took away the smallest tree, or if no tree came, we dropped two more seeds. Beside these and this spring we would set out strawberries which would bear well for three seasons and by then the peaches would bloom and would yield their first fruit. My father watched each tree grow and knew the heart of each one. They grew on him, to his knees, to his waist, to his head, and above him and on toward the sky. On the third year the north side held onto its snow and the south side let its snow melt sending small streamlets toward the larger stream in the valley. The frost came late but the blooms later and my father took from each tree a bloom and broke it apart and saw it was not black and would in autumn be a peach seasoned and ripened by the sun.

But that was long ago and now the fields are gone and the sprouts have turned to timber and there is only an echo hinting of what it was. On the highest ridge, overlooking all the other ridges and into all the valleys, stands a large black oak, its lower limbs all dead and gnarled and its higher limbs still reaching upward and green. Under the black oak lie five of my brothers and sisters and beside them my mother and father. They who had stood on this land and looked at this sky now rest here forever.

Lee Pennington

THE CLEARING

Lee Pennington

Barkley Dennis   *by Jill Baker*

Lee Pennington

MANCHILD

We first cleared the land, waded snow
deep on our coffee sack shoes
wrapped and tied about the feet
and knees to keep the cold away.

We first cut the trees, bright axes
pounding chips on the chill
sliding wedges till the swish down,
while we stood slapping limbs from the side.

We first plowed the land, tore roots
from mad man made rows of corn
and other green brought ripe
in the late October sun.

We first picked the fruit of vine,
worked tangled briars of berries
all purple and red dripping juice
on a manchild and a man.

We first cleared the land.
And now you lie in the quiet
wilderness where gnarled oaks and pines
sing a clinched fist wind.

BARKLEY DENNIS

Old Barkley Dennis sunk a plow
deep earthward hunting roots every spring
and turned out mostly rocks
whose skinned faces shined
like a hillside of baldheads after rain.

He came carrying potatoes
cubed into great dark eyes
saying planting time was according
to the gospel of Mr. Saint Patrick

and sometimes before green
would sink them deathly down
and faith not only to move mountains
but hold back frost

he'd get burned by guilty rot—
three hundred pounds of potato eyes
gone blind.

He'd finger the darkness out of earth
sometimes even taste the black breath
spitting out too many long hours
to gather loneliness.

Even his curse words full like eagle screams
didn't last longer than the sun
chasing dark tree shadows across the field.

Old Barkley Dennis would sink the plow again
trying to catch spring off guard
before the end.

Lee Pennington

SICKLE ARMED

Sickle armed and ragweed driven he
wakes upside down this sleepy day
breaks life untamed
leaves wild leaves lay.

Between swishing tumble
he hears a raven cry—
something he's not heard before
where shadows catch the eye.

He turns to see of sound this thing
hid beyond the dark wood's edge
and is in time for black wing folds
to mark the greyness of the ledge.

Moments later, that voice again—
center of darkness, cry after cry
as though this bird finds argument
where sickles swing, when wild weeds die.

BIRDS OVER THAWING LEOPARD SNOW

Birds over thawing leopard snow
above wishing grass;
love notes
sweep easy wind with sound of purple lilacs.

Shadows glow like ink stains,
fade flowers of a summer dress.
The limbs are casual—
locusts, oaks and redbuds
swing sky dark fingers.

Down by the eastern morning
loving horizon red
the sun slips against
the rattle-tat-tat of a woodpecker's head

over butterflies walking on bursting flowers
anxious feathers dream hours deep in wood.

Lee Pennington

BEANPOLES

First in winter we saw strange sassafras,
young and brown, rising up the mountain foot
like fingers of old men, and even in snow
they looked as wind scattered webs. You remember
them? Bean Pole Charlie who earned his name
eyed them too and saw each winter dead sapling
gold nuggets, or better still, rising stairs
formed, after the last plow, like Indian tents.
And he'd tell you of giant Kentucky pole beans
and Missouri wonders fat and green
that a half dozen would fill a peck basket,
and I guess it's worth remembering
that a long sharp corn knife, swung
in angles to flash the winter sun, almost
a signal for spring in Bean Pole Charlie's vision,
left stacks of them like long snakes,
and white-yellow teeth on the mouth of earth.

SEVEN SISTERS

Up from shade rising
the seven sisters bloom
by the old well pump
fragile as moss
and the ground squirrel
pauses as if to swear
on the odor slipping
lover-like with the wind.
The hemlock needles shed.
Blackbirds rush an
unnecessary noon.

Soon it will snow
a reddish-pink snow
a seven sisters snow

and such falling
hurried quickly close
to every bloom—

a downing
I've come to accept,
a sureness
I've come to know.

Lee Pennington

CORNFIELD

He went to the cornfield
with a gooseneck hoe
and couldn't see the ground
below the weed grow.

He left wilting necks
to dry in the sun
and slashed a trail wide
like wilderness undone.

He could not rest or think
till corn broke ground.
But a late July moon
turned shadows around.

BEYOND

Through the glass, three of six panes cracked,
beyond the dried bull thistle, birds fly
scattering January into pieces
of wings grey and brown. The tired, old
yard (capturer of leaves) hints of coming warm—
the rise of wild onions, the grass dried
but mirror enough of hemlocks beyond
to shadow green.

Limbs, dark with December, rise sharply
when birds lift and go, willing open
the waiting wind.
The japonica, forsythia threaten
early bloom.
Lilies, Easter named, spike up.

Hanging still in throat of winter
whispering spring breath,
these are the signs
not unlike rattle of death

TO BE

He wanted to be a carpenter
the finish kind driving nails home
against the grain, locking but
not splitting the wood.

But his worth, or bent as the family
would say, left him only enough
to guide a hoe against the weeds
not drive a nail blind

as he wanted half as much again
as anything. Still with no hope left
to think strings of steel into wood
and structured finish smooth as glass

he became the best with hoe he could
learning each new day to make a cleaner wider slash
until every swing down the hoe to hammer understood
building newground dreams from brushpile ash.

BLACKBIRD FRUIT

The morning of blackbird fruit
wings rainy way of spring
filling dark wintery trees
shattering the ice song.

Unexpected ripe darkness
(for who remembers bloom?)
such sudden growth and no
time for readying long reaching
ladders, no time for gathering,
cleaning empty baskets.

Who anyway can prepare
for strange fruit never bloomed?

It's there, simply there
like dreaming of sheep
and waking find
a roomful of wool.
How to pick an unplanned crop?
Decisions weigh more
than dark whispery feathers.

No need anyway.
One blush of wind
completes the whole
harvesting.

SOWING

Floyd Collins sowed seeds
flying finger tips
scissor cuts of dove wings
spraying evenly out
with a still wind
a soft fluttering down
hunting earth
haunting the last winter fall
or the first spring thaw
depending which direction
one stood.

Walking briskly
Water bucket full of seed
hung bail-wise at the elbow
his right hand dug in
spread rainbows out in front
ending each time
with five fingers like a fan
pointing up.

His long lines
laid straight as a furrow
each side pepper printed
each boot track deep and sure.

When the sun fell,
you could tell he'd
done it right, accurate
as a machine
but with one difference-
the knowledge of fingers
flesh fondling each handful
sensing future green.

HOW STILL THE NIGHT HOLDS ITS WEIGHT

How still the night holds its weight;
as if by dream fate
the torn moon catches ice
close of light—dice
snake eyes multiplied,
broken wisdom tried.

How without wind some sound
cracks above frozen ground
then quiet once more below—
language of lipless snow
silent again but speaking still,
a cat crouched before the kill.

How like the morning, strange
tracks stalk a pure range
of white, yet nowhere seen
mysterious herds searching green.
Bodiless feet make their mark
to claim a presence in the dark.

How stranger still frost born love
descends total darkness above
death to life, life to death
crystalized grey fog breath.
Angels rush; fools hesitate
where night quietly holds its weight.

THE LAND'S GREATEST GIFT

Lee Pennington

Rainbow Princess   *by Jill Baker*

Lee Pennington

EIGHTY SEASONS

His life limped across eighty seasons
nearly a thousand moons
before his eyes went gray
like swimming summer clouds—
eyes once accustomed to the polished
bead at the end of his twelve-gauge
long-tom, and even now squirrels
fall in great flashes of reds and grays
of a memory brought to its knees.

His listening, too, broke with his eyes,
and in his mind without proper reasons
he no longer joyed of fiddle tunes
lost like promises of yesterday
knowing all, between the quiets and louds
even linking thoughts abolished
and no dreams remembered enough for rage.
He had no special quarrels
wondering anyway what stays
broken under foot in December freeze.

He was torn from the same lands
that gifted him like some wingless bird
somehow yet flying the winter skies.

Still, I think he heard
young quail singing in his hands.

Lee Pennington

YOU, POETS

You, good people, are the poets—
rhyming with your hands and eyes,
and I could not say less if you dream
and build, and if you shape the earth.

I saw a man in mountain city walk on a big street
carrying his farm in calloused hands,
buying 5-10-10 to pay back the land.

I heard a man down by the river,
beyond the cliffs,
speak injustice, holding an arrow in his hand,
saying we wronged the red man, this was his land,
and I can't help but think so
burned in the leaves of Indian summer.

I saw a woman, torn with age, run
silver fingers through a quilt of many suns,
each stitch a footprint for her hands.

And another born with multicolored flowers
patching her mind, carrying rose odors
in gentle worn hands.

I saw a star fall and golden eyes catch its going
a child's eyes wind watching the world.

I saw an old man bent over a plow
following a mule, writing hillside lines.

And a woman's slender fingers stained with berries.

I saw a maker of chairs weave strips of hickory
bark into design singing songs of rest and half slumber.

I saw hands, torn and worn, white slender fingers
live with touch, hands building dreams
hands dreaming of building and you, good people,
are the poets.

RAINBOW PRINCESS

Rainbow Princess dances spring feet
picking up hurt limbs
fallen over winter's treat
of chill and wind chances.

Rainbow Princess sleeps with stars
swinging under trees and heaven
free of time's scars
when the great cloud weeps.

Rainbow Princess brings lips of love
whispered each touch morning
pale as the dove
in the song she sings.

Rainbow Princess blows off heads
of grey dandelions, flinging seeds
down into earth beds
and then she knows.

Rainbow Princess holds away the night;
when her color unfolds
she smiles out the light
in a field of marigolds.

PERLINA GINGER

Perlina Ginger aged like a cellar 'tater
sang the old songs
told the tales nearly lost
tied her money to a sack
locked it to her petticoat
drank a dram when she could
and longed for hell
where she wouldn't cut wood.

She couldn't read, she couldn't write
but followed weather well enough
each night, predicted storms
to come by colored flags
bright on the great wall calendar.

If she were here listening to whisper pines,
I know she'd say,
"There's going to be storm
come tomorrow."

The little back flag above her clay
whips in constant sorrow.

JAMES T

James T, the initial his own making
was a spitter—fine and accurate,
honed to an art—a good model
to lock ambition onto. On a 1934
Ford front seat mounted on bricks
on a poplar pole (set up too green
and splitting) porch he'd ride lazy summer
afternoons casting a strange dark eye
on a beat down bare yard (snakes you know)
looking for targets sometimes thirty,
forty feet away. The moving ones he liked
best—a challenge—no silent stone, no
dead twig but hoppers, crawlers and slow walkers.

Between the watch and wait he'd spin yarns
great wide ones truth thin halfway down
the valley, lies thick enough to charm
leaves, wake the frogs, make squirrels bark,
stop skippers on a dead creekbed stream.

That, too, an art but not so decidedly made.

As James T used to say, "Now it don't take
much practice to tell a good lie, but
spitting, why, that's a horse of a different
collar. First you got to learn to chew
and that don't come easy like walking or talking."

Remembering then my own first attempt
biting off a hard plug, sitting and swinging
on a bent young saplin and never quite
learning when to swallow, when to spit,
I judged him right on his estimation.

Sick enough to eat grass (I'd seen
dogs do that), I had to give up
my first ambition in life.

There have since been others—
some less noble, some reached and some
which left me ill as that first time.

But I supposed it doesn't hurt anything
to set your goals on spitting
even if you never learn to chew.
It gives you sort of a respect,
an admiration, for those that do

Like James T, fingers folded tight
against his lips, golden amber flying
through the air—a twang, a hiss,
and some bug drown in sting
wishing it'd stayed in the grass.

THIS GROUND

Charlie Blevins rides the hayrake today
rolling up waves of new cut grass,
back and forth with bold-brown hair
fixed and combed like a Tennessee woman.

He rides tall on the old iron machine
and makes each hand lift, drop perfect
rolls. The leather traces lie on his lap
like a shotgun. Charlie clicks at the horse,
blinks at the sun.

Two moons ago Charlie plowed this ground, threw
hay seeds on an easy wind, ran the soft black earth
through his fingers, stood looking at the birds
come down to eat the grain and out turned worms.

He was nearly finished, making his last crescent moon
swing, flinging pepper specks on air a moment suspended
in his stare, when across the new plowed dirt a voice
familiar carried to him like over water.

"Hey, Charlie!" and letting both hands drop, one
empty and the other holding the nearly shrunk seedsack,
Charlie turned, looked against the sun
across the field, saw Crate
form a word funnel with his hands.

"Hey, Charlie! They got your boy! Dean Gregg
and them has got your son and they'll kill
him sure. He's locked up in the smokehouse
and they're having fun with whip and gun!"

"Goddamn!" was all he said and let the seedsack
fall by his feet, let it drop and stay there
like the seeds caught in his stare, then followed
the sun back to his shack, his gun.

He rolled the chamber of this Thirty-Eight
and found it like he knew, found it full,
then guided it under his belt and pulled
his faded blue coat to hide the bulge.

"Dean, I've come to get my boy! Now turn
him loose. I don't want any foolishness." Charlie's
hat brim ears picked up the sound from the shadows,
heard Dean Gregg form a plan.

"I'll shake his hand," Gregg said to the tall one.
"When I get his hand, you drop him from the back.
Old Charlie will scare as quick as his son.
We'll lock him up too and have some fun."

"Dean, I want my boy. That's why I've come."
"Hell, Charlie. I want to be your friend;
I'll shake your hand."
Charlie bit his lip,
pulled out his gun.

"I heard you, Gregg. I heard every word you said. Take one
more step and by God you're dead!"

"Hell, Charlie, I'm your friend. I shake your hand.
I'm a mean sonofabitch but I'll shake your hand."

"By God!" Charlie said but the end sound
was gone, lost in the roar of his Thirty-Eight.
Gregg went down, straight back and down,
his eyes wide through blue smoke and sound.

The tall one at Charlie's back ran through the weeds.
Charlie watched him go, then filled his belt
again with bulge, pulled his coat around,
walked to the smokehouse and got his son.

When the hay was done, raked and rolled,
and lay smelling in the sun, Charlie
Blevins looked across the field, liked it all—
The ripe hay cut down in early fall.

DON'T RIDE CHARLIE

Don't ride Charlie;
he ain't no pony.
He's a little nickel man
standing on the corner
gonna shine shoes for somebody
so you can see your face in 'em.

Why, he's the best shiner you've seen.
Got all that black stuff and poppin' rag
and a little stand to foot on
while he goes, pop pop pop.

No, not Charlie! You!
Charlie can't see his face;
he's black too.

Lee Pennington

ORVILLE WINSTON

Orville Winston, tall and bendy back,
chased every dawn including Sunday
across the day, burning brush
and turning plow and fearing
every smoke rise Sabbath
the prison moon.

Still he burned reasoning such fire
stronger need than superstition
real as real wicked or no
the time for work all time
the time to burn and plow and sow.

Some say his crops
carried the devil's tail
that corn whispered magic in the night.
Others just that Sunday burning
was the lowest low
and the Great Harvester would set it right.

Orville Winston breathed the crazy wind,
held the flames as best he could at bay
but too much smoke, too many Sundays,
they found his ashes with the crippled wood—
both a ghostly grey.

Now the old timers, as a stern warning
to the young, point to the dark shading
of every fall, say nearly with a hush:
"There's old Orville Winston, the moon man,
caught that fatal Sunday burning brush."

Lee Pennington

LINE

It is a long line, and when the front car
pulls onto the gravel road, there will be
a wait for the other end to draw in.
Then onto the plain dirt road now heavy
with thaw, shadows of willow green
riding on hoods where humming mud
has not replaced the shine.
Tracks grow deeper now—deeper than you
have ever known in any spring.
You can hear the scraping, dragging,
and wheels spinning off rubber
smells. The tracks have no bottoms,
and the line has no end.

EARTH POET

The way he broke earth
he knew a strong binding
subtle as stone worth.
He gave space along winding

roads leading into dark hills
to land claimed new each
generation—great sprout kills
when stump shoots reach

up green as fingers.
The way he held soil
hand wise, loam lingered
memory black of such toil,

the labor no less love.
Plow following, he wrote lines
strange as swirling clouds above
ridges rich with tall pines.

Each season one more chapter,
his life an unread book.
What he tamed, now tames him—
laughter—the final wilderness look.

Lee Pennington

WHEN THE LEAVES TURN GREEN

I saw a man who cleared new land
and watched the brush piles burn.
I saw him plow and plant by hand
with faith that leaves would tum.

He often cleared his head of sweat
with the swipe of his knotty hand,
and searched for truth not in the sky
but in the rocks and sand.

From this land I saw the man
come to the end of his row
and lean heavy on the back of
a skinny gooseneck hoe.

I saw this man through winter last
wait like the seeds of earth
to time his rendezvous with death
when all the plants gave birth.

MUSIC REMEMBERED

Lee Pennington

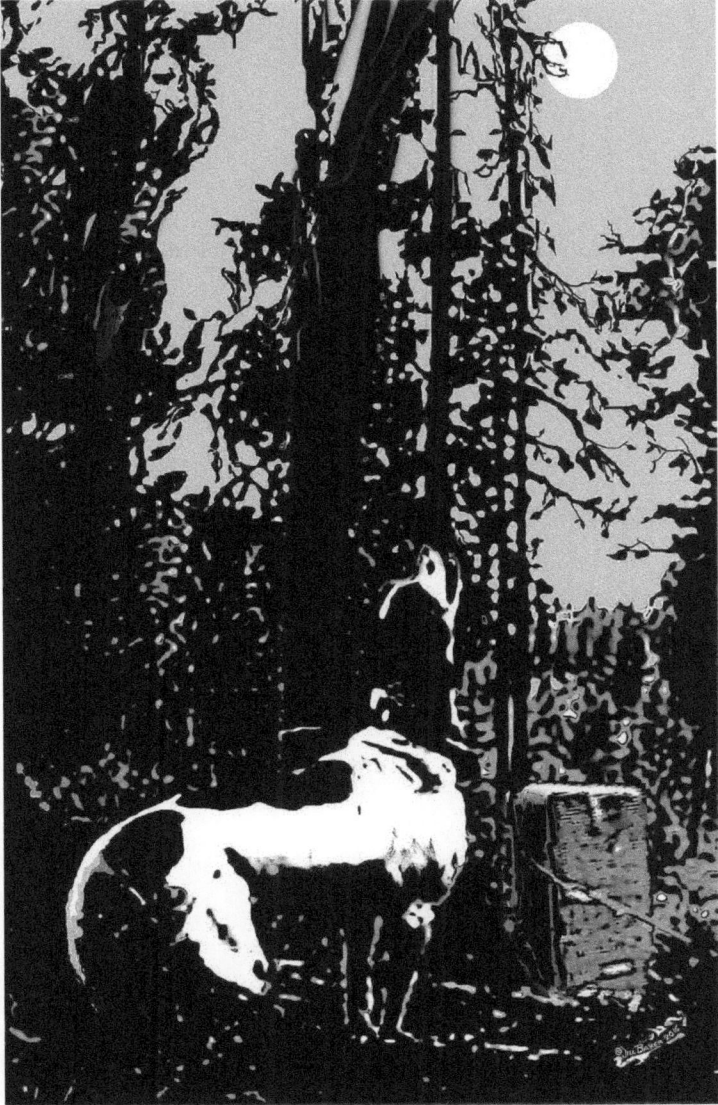

Old Ben   *by Jill Baker*

Lee Pennington

HOLD ON

Hold onto your dream;
don't ever let it get away.
Too many once dreamers,
silent with nothing to say,

stagger through what's left
of life, drunk on cheap death,
drink no more rich life wine
which gives us breath.

So what if you never reach
What you're always reaching for.
The dream alone is enough,
Perhaps even more.

So hold onto your butterfly.
Stain your hands where colors pass.
A dreamless soul walks
barefoot on broken glass.

OLD BEN

We lost old Ben last week and Mom
said she guessed he'd got to chasing
sheep and someone loaded him down
with number-three buckshot. I walked
the ridges with the old doublebarrel
and looked for him—breaking down
the gun and lifting red foxhorn
sounds across the wind, but he didn't come.

I looked for him three days in a row
and then had to get back to work—
the weeds were taking over the farm.

Sunday I went back again. I figured
Mom was right—old Ben always came home
for his biscuits. I guessed he was
either dead or hung up in some wire or vines.
If he were dead, I wanted to bury
his bones. I looked all day
but couldn't find him.

It was Friday, that was a week ago yesterday,
and I got a late start on the milking
and didn't get finished until way late.
I went down to the creek and washed the day's
dust off and then went straight to bed.

I reckon it must a been sometime after midnight
when Mom woke me up.
"Listen, Tad," she said.
"I think that's old Ben a howling. Listen.
Can you hear him?" I heard him all right.

My God, what a lonesome sound. I never
heard old Ben howl like that before. I
got up right away, got my pants on and went
to the barn to get the lantern. The sound
was coming from Tall Ridge and I had an awful
time trying to beat the underbrush
to get back there. I had blackberry briar
scratches all over me.
I found him and I couldn't believe my eyes.
I called to him but he acted like he didn't
even know me. I thought he was mad at first.
They's been a lot of foxes around that's gone
mad and the health officials in Greenup
told us to be mighty careful with our dogs.

But he wasn't mad. He was just your dog.
He stood there by your grave
a howling at the wind—a sound
long as eternity.

Lee Pennington

SAILING STONES

He stood skipping stones,
sensing delight of good sailers
with a rattlesnake twist of the wrist
and a flying fish's eye,
to turn it just right on the wind
to lay flat against the deep still pool,
a stone dipping and diving
coming alive in its motion,
and only a good sailer could have,
or hold, such devotion.

BIRDS IN FLIGHT

Somewhere back near the dawn
delicate fingers, I picture them
white flesh bones, cut brown birds
and with thread sewed a sky
full of feather flight, winging
their way in design of a night cover.
I think, too, gentle old eyes
looked into the cloth of Appalachia,
tore from the heritage of hands
a common art, yet each thread
made it real, made it individual,
still not knowing where the birds
in subtle patterns would fly.

Lee Pennington

BEYOND THE FOREST

The forest holds the world, your world,
around the dark. Beyond the mystery
there is sound full and round
akin to moonglow, akin to honey
fanned sweet by wings-
love moans from forgotten flowers.

Sound precious as raindrops
hides in teeth caught between
scream and delight beyond
the forest beyond the dark
waiting like wind
waiting like water.

Mother Goddess, I have seen
your forest touched your dark
to singing found your honeymoon
danced your night to song.

I have heard whisperings of you
sure as squirrels jumping in dawn-
wet-leaves, sending droplets down.
I have seen a blind man's vision.
I have heard a deaf man's sound.

BEGGARS

I love beggars
ever since the old blind one
of my youth stood on the hot streets
of Portsmouth
with a tin cup tied to the end
of a Harmony guitar
and a French harp tied around a red veined neck
sang "Jesus, I'm Coming Home"
and I dropped a quarter
music enough in the cup
and the sound blended one
note of Jesus music
cup music
Harmony guitar twang
French harp whine
and the sound of a smile
carved deeply on an age ridden face.

THE POET

He never had a pen, at least
not the kind with ink,
nor paper either, for that
matter. Still, he was a poet.
I heard him say as much.
He waited for the rain
and with a stick traced lines
where fallen weather left
brown puddles for his hand.
And the lines rose up like
rolling clouds where tadpoles
leave swimming trails of small
tails swinging them along.
The brown waters wrote his song.
Until one bright and not so sunny day
a speeding truck splashed his lines away.

FREIGHT TRAIN

Don't tell me I didn't see it
down along the Ohio River
with shiny rails laying atop
rough smelling crossties
beside too-many-wires on telephone poles.
Don't tell me I didn't hear the whistle humming
and come barefoot running
to feel the vibration
shaking my toes, rocking my soul!
Don't tell me I didn't have to wipe
cinders from my red eyes
to see the smoke stack split open
and spread out over the river
making it jump
drunk with butterflies.

BIRD SONGS

Out of night such waters come
washing bird songs away—
a claim of April, I assume,
soaking music into clay.

Down down and down
below the wind
the earth bursts brown
smiles, another time to mend

sorrow sounds of winter.
Up up comes green—
each blade a living splinter
dark from darkness clean.

The birds, then, are the ones
cut by rain's great knife,
willing when spring comes
to trade their songs for life.

ROCKING CHAIRS

I get lonely sometimes
when I see a long line of rocking chairs
stretched out like a sleepy cat's paw
along some porch where wind
grabs hold of backs and
starts the sand brown empty seats
to rocking.

I get feeling deep inside,
down and empty like the rocking chairs
as they swing back and forth
while one or two
sit motionless
in the wind.

ECHOES

They return like dog howls in misty dark—
shouts past rested rise and ride
back this way; rumbling
hoofs peck away like sharp glass
like whiskered frost breaks from grass.

I hear them on restless nights—
tumbling ghosts speak out of dreams
like a humming fly, a spider's wish.

I hear whispers like my own
footfalls re-lifting their sounds
to follow my walking back down.

Like fog on the wind.
Like frogs leaping from lily pads
where splashed water curls on itself again.

CRY COLOR

Cry color for the day is new
spread lawns in morning sun
and clouds shock the blue
change a flower noon.

Cry black for the day is here
broken highways ribbon thin.
Brick building windows fear
wet faces of wrinkled men.

Cry Red for the day is old
closing like morning glory seeds
turn flower, each pet a fold
on bent wind against river reeds.

Cry white for the day is gone
down the highway of rising moon.
Katydids like green upon shadows
singing the final tune.

Lee Pennington

AGAIN A TRAIL

I know I've walked this trail before
searching thoughts could understand.
Today my eyes take in much more
of things connected to this land.

I breathe new air clean as grass
squint to see where sunlight goes.
I look at hills that never pass
search for wind that never blows.

These memories I have are cold and grey—
winds ripping at spindly trees
forcing autumn on its way
filling air with colored leaves.

Now a thousand jarflies sing
the song of death that frost will bring.

SAY, WON'T YOU REMEMBER

Say, Carl, won't you remember
Beech Creek and our gone banjo
hunting? I mean down that
snake road and them tall bone
back mountains, the sun on the tops
like hounds sounding a hot trail.
And wasn't it something standing
in that wood loved place,
(and where was old Guy?)
seeing that minds and hands
had turned trees into art
as ancient as old Elk talking
on the stones down through Pogie?
You might just as well have taken
one of them laurel gumslings down
and shot the whole thing through my heart—
the hickory brooms,
(or were they scrub mops?) and the cedar canes
(did I come back with one?) which looked
snakes to me, and that lonely dulcimer
And what about that woman built like
a tough hide hickory who told of snaking
logs and making whimmy diddles (or whatever
they're called) and coming back
you said old Ider plowed, and I thought
good looking women here are something
grubbing stumps and making love and some say
they've always been that way.

CRICKETS

You can hear them on a cold morning
before dawn, chattering like rising
chickens, but you have to listen
hard and make like you're just passing.
The minute you stop and show yourself
aware, the singing is done; they stop
and wait, wait for you to move on.
I suppose they must somehow feel it wrong
to sing any but an unpretentious song.

OLD BARN

An old barn fighting the wind
is a plenty. Rusty nails now
bare as late November fields
with nearly weed stubble growth.
The racket is enough to frighten
Birds—old boards banging.

Where are those men these ghosts
now mock? Where are the mules
of empty stalls? Now the hayloft
falls into a home for rats and owls.
Rotting eaves with the roof blown
back and wasps sprinkled like raisins
across the undersides.

A musty, leather smell
and rattling chains of empty harnesses.
Broken singletrees left for rain
beside the plow points noisy hanging.

An old barn fighting the wind
is a plenty.

Lee Pennington

LADY SEWING SONGS

Lady, your fingers talk blackbirds
clip violets from the dark stillness
stitch love bright willing patterns
sunrise eyes above yes whispering willows.

You slip through, songs break memory
to crying, laughter to greening
and wildflower purple dance among May
as lying deep in lilacs
dreams wake the mind's river.

Flinging songs bloom flower wise
and thread sure, you touch bee wings
to sing a sweet working
a poetry, an art,
a moon honey heart.

DRINKING WATER LOVE SONG

Long necked blackbirds sing
the drinking water love song,
swing swallowing
to tell a lover wet sound.

One stretches his neck
catches light on black
makes sliding rainbows.

Dark clouds gather wind
blackbirds hang on wing suspend
loving in air.

Rainwater
is the voice of love
drenching spring
somewhere.

Lee Pennington

BLUE MOON

Where the blue moon is down
against stone grey and cold
I wait for spiders to bring
frost colored webs.

I wait where blowing wind
makes poetry of leaves;
high above a young fur thing
shade-nest scatters
sound enough to plant a different song.

I am tempted to think all music
being romantic and weak
but these growing things are not
violin strings and no
master's hand strokes
the blue moon fall.

It's the glass colored wind
caught in trees;
that's all.

GENTLY BEYOND WINTER

Spring shoved March early this year
and it would have been your season
to talk in warm distant winds
to run dark earth through old hands
to measure what's left of love.

It would have been your season
to welcome wake of leaves on sad grey trees
to break soil, plant seeds,
gamble on the last silent frost.

But it's only an early spring, a reminder,
green spirits hovering on a land
now ten seasons lost.

OF EARTH

I remember spring of year
when she went to fields of growing corn
and on her knees in fresh plowed earth
placed her ear to stalks to hear
young blades born.

Once the snow came late.
April blooms died; death was cold
she came weeping from winter's delay
carrying on her back the load
of the world white and dead.

Now she too must hear the wind—
finally being so much of earth—
the hemlock needles whet against stone
and leafless limbs moan
where moonlight gives shadows birth.

THE ONE ROAD IN

I am here among the country dead
where paths succumb to wilderness—
sawbriars, grapevines, sassafras instead
have taken over this hill and now express

the longing of dark shadows underneath.
I came across the road you made by hand.
I lay on your mound a wilted wreath.
Now briars and weeds have command.

I remember when a dozen paths and roads
found their way clean on this jutted hill.
Now all save one are left for snakes and toads
which crawl under green growing still.

Here the first road in was the last.
Now the sun cannot reach the ground.
The whisper winds all are winds of past,
and blowing here is a lonesome sound.

Lee Pennington

WE WAKE IN NIGHTMARE

Lee Pennington

Sprouts (Man Entangled)   *by Jill Baker*

Lee Pennington

SPROUTS

One day we cleared them out you and I
with gooseneck hoes and mowing scythes.
Now these sprouts have turned to timber
tall enough for limbs low wind sighs.

How strange to find them now
here surrounded by oaks and pines—
full grown trees from stumps
scattered in broken patterned lines.

But stranger still
is how you let them grow
let them whip you in the rage of night—
their roots tearing at your body so.

Lee Pennington

WIND BONES

Today the wind has bones.
They rattle from mud tracks
limbs
stubbles in fields
bee wings.

White and bleached
unsaturated by meat.

Far flung and restless
as time. Broken as thoughts
in moving atmospheres.

Today the wind has bones.
The skeletons walk as whispers
and make gestures beyond the senses.

AUGUST

Down the road he comes humped over
like a coat-hanger on a rusty nail
bent in a building side. One wonders
why the old man never fell

with so many chances: a stumble here,
a trip there, just enough on balance
to remain erect. A witch's pot or eye
must hold him up in a kind of trance.

He stands there embarrassed,
not knowing where to go;
his red face offers only a mocking blush
to dull skies of migrating crow.

But blue evenings are only echo shadows
walking on a blind man's cane
whispering new color to sucking leaves
that will not stay green in spite of rain.

BLEEDING MOMENTS

I cannot know the hours
torn red beside waiting—
hearing crazy roosters crow
feeling sleeping flesh restless.
Hounds howl the night
while the moon is dark
and old men lie in the cup
of their underarm thinking love
dreaming hot passion days
gone south for winter.
Fireflies flash a mocking yes
above each instant, one million
yellow night eyes winking
and I cannot know such hours.
For time is my lost fingers touching
notes of a lonely guitar
where Every American Daughter
must do it all
for the last three strings
are missing.

SNAKE SPIT

Where are the crawling snakes this dawn?
Where in the dark have they gone?

In woods white foam hangs misfit.
Someone told me it's snake spit.

I also see it clinging wet in grass
wonder how many snakes had to pass

to leave so much themselves here today.
I'd say perhaps a hundred came this way.

And I wonder why I stand here staring so
intently at the path where night snakes go.

VOICE

This night with weak winds
brings back minds tangled
like barbwire in thickets
a voice clear as bones
drying on the ridge. It is
silence screaming.
Birds fly but cannot know
restless trees below.
It is forever this subtle claim
of stones marked awkwardly
over the dead—
the things left unsaid.

WINTERS

The winters slip up on us—
redbud winter dogwood winter
blackberry winter—come
from bloom a trick of chill
to catch us off our guard
even when we know.

Not like the Big Winter-
the "Main One" old Clyde says—
that flings away leaves
torn with color,
readies us open and fair
for cold ripping wind
for white dance down
for freeze cracking stones.

There's a Big Winter in life,
according to Clyde,
who's watched a plenty
come and go
and says we shouldn't
carry on so if and when.

With chill from every bloom
we've been prepared ahead
enough times not to dread.

CROW SONG

Old crow sing your lonesome song
black feathers darker than water.
Wild bird know all is lost,
chill coming on south bound wing,
your love song of time gone
now to tame you the frost.

You chase the last leaves swooping down.
You mock them with love notes of spring
unmindful of weather ways
where nothing, even nothing, ever stays.

You sing final caw caws to some missing lover—
now your dreams far away as the crow flies
with too much wind and miles in your eyes.

ISLANDS

The leaves have reached maximum
endness. Yesterday they fell.
Each on a near silent lisp or hum
went spacedown in a witch's spell.

No other thrust can rip them
from limbs again. Now they rest,
islands in themselves, no requiem.
They are no more, no less than dust.

No different from brown grass
whose skins whisper new sounds.
All like supernatural foxfires pass
to lesser fungus of undergrounds.

Lee Pennington

THE BET

Old Red was sucking wind.
His bark came from Pilot Ridge.
John said the fox had reached his end,
at least was somewhere near the edge

Clyde was the first to raise dissent.
He laid a silver dollar on the ground.
Right off, John did not know what it meant—
he sat there, blank-eyed, not a sound.

"I call you, John," said Clyde
with hand-cupped ear.
John ran his hand deep into his pocket
and pulled two dollars, smiled right queer,
sat there wondering if Clyde would top it.

Three dollars sparkled near the fire.
Clyde fetched two more, kissed them with a grin—
flipped them out like a double shooting star,
then waited for the other betting man.

On and on that night the waging went.
The silver dollars shined on the dirt.
Steel grey eyes, smiles down bent.
John wiped his sweaty hands across his shirt.

He could hear Old Red a barking long—
his voice moved across the autumn leaves
and floated back this way soft as song.
John paused, rolled up his sleeves.

We heard the fox's shrill falling cry,
then deep silence on the chilly night.
John raised up, closed a single eye.
"Something's wrong," he said. "It don't sound right.

I trained Old Red. He wouldn't stop running.
He'd die first." John shook his head.
Hot coals on the fire had stopped burning.
"It just ain't right. I know Old Red."

He lit the lanterns, we climbed around the hill,
around to Devil's Den above tall Hanging Cliff.
Our clomping feet raised a whippoorwill.
"The Devil's sign!" shouted wild-eyed Jeff.

John climbed below, put the lantern on the ground.
Pale yellow light painted dog and fox.
John said he'd bury them both fox and hound
here where they came together on the rocks.

Lee Pennington

THE HOUNDS ARE RESTLESS

The hounds are restless their minds
clouded moons where dark wild
runs in blood moves in veins
cool as wind.

The muddy red river rips
their brains. They stare and bark
in a mountain wilderness—
noses lifted in the dark.

Something out there where trees
close the fields in.
They can't see it but they know.

Inside their eyes dark rivers splashing.
Inside their minds a wild afterglow.

WIND

I took for my bedfellow the wind;
but he kept shifting off the covers.
Mad as sin I cursed his eyes
and heard him drag off heard his bones
rattle through the underbrush.
I did not know a man could hurt the wind.
I did not know that breezes have pride.
If I could I would call him back again—
this wind which crawled off somewhere and died.

Lee Pennington

THE FLOWERS HAUNT ME

The flowers haunt me blow back empty
milkwood blooms already white hair
seeds have gone flying.
I have broken spring green stems
felt the milk juice drip sticky
around my fingers stain me yellow
while goldenrod sticks mock the meadow.
And the wild blackberry blooms
bring back winter cool frost days before June
down where the wild snakes are crawling.
Daisies, too, tease the wind,
then go make love to earth
and the wind keeps blowing.
I watch wild red eyes hiding in grass
and momma's gonna make a shortcake
but not of these.
The corn has just broken through
And lies in long green lines from a distance.
Be a long hot day in July
before silks fall like a woman's hair
down beside the spider roots
where flowers haunt me,
and the wind keeps blowing.

EARTHWARD

As a child
I took in my hand
bird eggs robin blue
and crushed till yellow red
ran down my fingers
and my father
already fifty seasons gone
wept at life not getting born.

As a child part man
I chased a squirrel
watched its frightened movement
in the trees jump from limb
to limb then settle in the leaves
to hide from gun and death;
still I brought him to earth
quivering down forever
and I wept.

As a man
I loved you delicate flower
wild in the youth fields
your bloom forever surprise
shadows in my eyes
till rose fingered and
willfully I tore you
from the earth
and know now
your worth.

BROKEN MIRROR,
THE SEVEN YEARS

Lee Pennington

Junkyard   *by Jill Baker*

Lee Pennington

JUNKYARD

They stand there battered chunks of metal
proud enough to reflect broken sun.

On a chilly morning or a wind whipped afternoon
you can walk among them and knee high
spirits will rattle the doors and honk the horns

and grey creatures scuttle
along the running boards and across hoods—
broken glass and crystal sounds flying from their feet.

IF I SEEM TO YOU LIKE BLUE GLASS

If I seem to you like blue glass
holding thoughts quiet as water
say the leaves now turn rainbow
a sacred promise that we've come
mountain wise to stop drifting.

Say the color sounds like wind
blowing all ages where we've never
been and now two by two
down from stranded love

the oceans become rivers
the land, land again
and together we wait
at daybreak's pass
seeming to you like blue glass.

WHO CARES?

Who cares she said
with coal eyes on a whole
world's undoing.
The young white dressed
virgins sacrificed
on smiling grey lips.
Who cares if
dragon teeth eat
away our rags
tear to flesh
our boneless spirits?
Who cares if
time turns on the head
of grey dandelions
twists all the agony
and outrage from us
till we sit cutting
the final paperdolls
from children's laughter?

Lee Pennington

BEFORE THE BREAKING

When my father spoke in his natural voice
he made babies cry
and that perhaps is the reason why
I stood my ground some distance from his dream
and never fully understood his hidden
gentleness dark like distant rivers
climbing against the midnight sun.
Never knew, I say, until night
ripped it all away and rough
course hands held the wind at bay
before the breaking of the storm
above where my father lay.

COOL NIGHTS

There will be cool nights.
Waiting on new spring we
will move as silent lights
across some winter sea.

There will be grass haunting
April stealing sometimes the dream
and later awakened on the hill
when the morning sun beam

drives a shaft into our lies
we will rub our palms
bent armward and our eyes
alternating storms and calms.

There will be cool nights
waiting, waiting always the wait.
We will move as silent lights
never to hesitate.

There we will know all love
deep cool nights, when death
too soon that hour above
comes to rob us of our breath.

Lee Pennington

CROW FEEDER

He saved corn for the crows
spoke words with bony hands
pointed behind green eyes staring
out across snow down mountains
at yellow stalks rising
upward yet bent to weight
of heavy heads drooped
like a sleepy chicken's.

He knew inward
having more than guessed
the toll of seasons
dark wonderful winters
where crows skinned
back blond heads
to get the grain.

He measured the corn stained fields
waving bony fingers
against the sky tall as autumn
saying half the distance there
was the crows' and his there beyond.

He raised long arms
above his head
each hand a tight fist
and let them fall again
dark hands against the sky

enough to make one think
the arm a stalk of corn
the hand a dark crow
riding the stalks down
again beside his side.

At night the crows
flew around in his head
and laughed their mocking cries
as if the grain of corn
grew somewhere in his dreams.

When he died
they tore the flesh
from his talking finger bones
plucked out his eyes
and laughed their mocking cries.

RED DOGWOOD

The time, I said, will come when the dogwood
will turn red to mark us halfway through
it all. Yet little did I know or could
back then way back then that blue
memories change their color, too. And how
perhaps more important than a dogwood red
or being half way there it is somehow
the feeling of leaves here all painted dead
and the mystery of a new beginning. Still
I would not have it so; I would take the half
and finish first. Seems too much the will
and way of every start to finish half a path
then begin anew. I notice that red leaves fall;
the dogwoods go from green to red is why.
I could think soft green but that's not it at all.
I think stark winter arms against the sky.

DARK BIRDS

"There must be a better way
to kill blackbirds other than
using a detergent to wash away
 their wax and oils."
(overheard in a conversation)

Oh black wings weighing winter sun
searching dreams beyond the poison wet
you fly from warm to warm as if inside
something knows self labyrinth.
Clouds cannot hold you, nor trees heavy
without leaves, nor fields of corn
silent of cicadas, emptied by your thrust.
They fear your voice in numbers
sung beyond song into scream,
fear your dark gathering
flying as you swallow shadows
till you are the night
holding away the light.
Ah, dear friends in ice death
you fly too close to earth.

FACE

The old tree, bent on the lap of the river,
had (from an ancient fallen limb) an empty face—
no eyes, no nose, nor mouth—a knothole face
bare and smooth, waiting beside the clear
naked plastic brought by high water love.
He looked at the empty face, resting his own
in hand, thinking he'd carve out a god (as
men will do) giving it a mouth, a nose, and eyes,
believing he could fill a void with face
and he moved such bringing the knife open
touching his thumb on the blade's sharpness
almost breathing out a headshake yes.
First the mouth (for gods must speak) and even
before it could see it smiled beside the river.
Then the nose he guessed could smell
the coming rain. Then eyes narrow and deep as if
too much sun burned in.
He stared and it stared, at him, or maybe
the river way and him between the staring,
a god carved on a faceless face.

The rest was record carved back on
his own face or deep behind mirrors;
his mind would grow around it
like woodflesh heals around roots
of fallen limbs makes a lip around empty faces.
He knew the weather warm bringing spring
deep out of the earth,

and he knew the sap up,
and he knew he carved the left eye too deep.

He accepted that.

Still there was that face,
and his face,
and the one carved behind his face

and the god was crying.

DREAMS OF ICE

Blackbirds gather east of November
strange fruit darkly ripe
mocking spring where leaves go down
searching a way back through hidden roots.

Giving limbs wake without wind
they startle stillness into song
and singing still distant from buds breaking
they drive screams into the wood.

Screams to claim a season beyond winter's chill
as if the chatter is a gathering of knife blades,
not birds, cutting to pieces dreams of ice
wounding weather where the sun bleeds.

DARKNESS, YES

Darkness comes
on green winds
tiptoeing each shadow
near quiet water.
Sheds sound on banks
covered with chiseled rock.
Water carved night
of nearly slick statue
nearly on restless feet
splashing a new face
from the dead stillness
the dead silent
curling on itself
of a whiskered horizon
licking the last shadow
from its paw
night closes by the river
speaks last to the stone.

KENTUCKY LUCKY

You go ahead and talk about Kentucky
about black winter buzzards flying in your eyes
and I'll tell you, you don't have kin
left around anymore to hear you speak.
I helped bury Clyde Dillow last week.
His sons are Dayton men, now just Dayton men,
and don't you stand there acting like it's a surprise.
If sons can't claim their dad, he ain't lucky.

You just tell me how roots go down deep
in this gulley forsaken earth, this coal sucked land,
and how Lexington highbrows love niggers in the street,
and I'll say, by God, ain't that sweet.
Makes me want to lick the ground
and kiss a race horse's feet.
Maybe you don't like the sound?
Maybe you'll tell me go dig a hole in the sand,
crawl inside for a long night's sleep?

Listen, I've heard talk since I could hear.
I hoed a steep hill against the July sun.
I guess I know pains in the ribs and on shins
a broken arm couldn't bring. I know roots
and every fog horn talker who toots
and every coward who drops his pants to run
and every farmer picking nubbins to fill corn bins.

But I'm not afraid. Not now. Anymore I can't fear.
It's like my wife said, what's to fear now?
We've fed our lives to the lions more than twice.
We've had dynamite at our backs for years.
We've watched bullets crack the bark of trees.
We've seen mules die at the plow.
We've seen enough broken women pay the price.
You just let the yellow clay soak up your fears;
not me. They can scare me cold, but I'll not freeze.

So you go ahead and talk and have your say.
You tell 'em about horses and highbred grass.
You tell 'em Abe Lincoln walks here on Sunday
and good folks get out to hear him pass.
And I'll show you barefoot blood prints in the snow.
I'll show you some people dying to feed the gutter.
I'll show you a thousand faces wanting love
while you turn your head away and point above.
Don't give me that God will help; it's sour butter.

Lee Pennington

DARK SMELL

This night smells of Appalachia
Dark Eden earth spilled in a coal dust sun
seeping like the milk of your face into rains
counted tracks cracking from coal dust wheels
from coal truck wheels and two eyed dragon
food rolling on the line, child of blackness
whimpering at each curve, whispering sudden
echoes on otherwise foreboding silence
white silence of a baby's hand
green silence of a mother's eye
black silence of a father's misery
and the dark bird, black bird, red-
winged black bird silence inside
a coal miner's mind watching rats
scampering on grey feet pulling long
grey hairless tails silent rats dancing
from the pits
before the final slatefall.

LAUREL

Searching the dark laurel where eyes stare
back and crawling sounds of a creature
long and black and milky white
underside like driftwood sticks
underfoot but more of scratching
leaves several winters deep.

Searching the dark laurel where grey
chestnuts lie rotting, castles of worms
working art of dying wood
windows or eyes on time's face
in love with greenbriars wrapped
in a lover's knot with perfect thorn.

Searching the dark laurel for shadow
footprints of an ancient damp world
of stones eons water and winter carved
of deep blue green mystery of wolves
howling babies crying wind dancing
in sun going down on the last moment.

Lee Pennington

BEYOND THE DREAM

Lee Pennington

Ragweed (Gravestones)   *by Jill Baker*

Lee Pennington

RAGWEED

Dramatist Personae

    Hand

    Foot

    Ragweed

Setting

A graveyard with three tall stones side by side center stage, these stones much taller than the others. No figures are on stage when the play opens. Music (guitar only) of the song "Ragweed" is softly playing in the background. It is night but there is moonlight, accented blue. Figures move onto stage one at a time and each stands behind one of three tall stones: first Hand from stage left, then Foot from stage right, then Ragweed from stage center.

HAND: (*To others*) Good evening.

FOOT & RAGWEED: (*Togethe*r) Good evening.

HAND: It's a lovely night. No, that can't be right. How can the nights anymore be lovely?

FOOT: Somewhere, to someone, it is a lovely night.

RAGWEED: Perhaps.

HAND: The night is never lovely, not by itself, and yet, that's all there is.

RAGWEED: To us?

HAND: To everyone.

FOOT: The moon is lovely.

RAGWEED: To us?

HAND: To everyone?

FOOT: To someone.

HAND: Somewhere the night with the moon is lovely to someone.

RAGWEED: Perhaps.

FOOT: Well, anyway, the night is.

HAND: The night is what?

FOOT: It just is.

HAND: It can't be just is. It has to be something.

RAGWEED: Perhaps.

HAND: Where have you been, Foot?

FOOT: Walking. What about you?

HAND: Holding.

RAGWEED: What about me? (*They both look strangely at Ragweed but say nothing*). I say what about me? (*They only stare. Ragweed clears throat*).

HAND: Must be hay fever.

FOOT: Yes.

HAND: Oh, let's ask him anyway.

FOOT: All right.

HAND AND FOOT: (*Together*) Where have you been, Ragweed?

RAGWEED: (*Smiling*) Spreading. (*Hand and Foot shrug*))

HAND: (*Looking around graveyard*) Do you think we should meet here every time?

FOOT: (*Shaking head yes*) It's the only place we all know.

RAGWEED: I know all places. (*Hand and Foot look angrily*)

HAND: Let's pretend we didn't hear that.

FOOT: Let's.

RAGWEED: (*Head down*) I'm sorry. (*Hand and Foot shrug*)

FOOT: No need. We're all beyond all that now.

HAND: Besides, even if it's the only place, it's not a bad place.

RAGWEED: Let's talk about before.

HAND: All right. I'll start. (*Looks up to night sky as if thinking, preparing an oration*) Those were the days. (*Long pause*)

FOOT: You're taking too long.

HAND: Always in a hurry. You ready?

FOOT: No.

HAND: (*To Ragweed*) You ready?

RAGWEED: I'm always ready.

HAND: Give me time. I'm thinking.

FOOT: (*Starts laughing*)

HAND: Now what?

FOOT: You said, "Give me time." (*More laughter*)

HAND: What's wrong with that?

FOOT: You've got to eternity. Do you think you'll need any more than that?

HAND: I forgot.

FOOT: No matter. There's plenty of time to remember.

RAGWEED: Yes, and to forget again.

HAND: (*In agreement, shaking head yes*) And to remember again.

FOOT: Over and over.

RAGWEED: I thought we were going to talk about before.

HAND: (*Remembering*) Yes. Those were the days. Then I thought I could do it all.

FOOT: Then you didn't know it all.

HAND: But I thought. (*Looks at hands held air*). These were the answer, the only one. They could hold a hammer, a plow, guide songs from a guitar, carve faces from the silent stone.

RAGWEED: (*Pointing to stones*) And names.

FOOT: Hold a knife.

HAND: It didn't matter and still I wonder. I am what these are.

FOOT: You are what they do.

RAGWEED: Touch. No more than a wet dishrag.

HAND: (*Glaring*) My all. (*Looking at hands now held down*) Build and shape, destiny controlled.

RAGWEED: You forget the night. Did you hold the night?

HAND: As surely as I held the wind.

RAGWEED: (*Smiles*) The wind, my constant lover.

HAND: You are all lover.

RAGWEED: I am all over (*smiles*)

FOOT: Let Hand tell his story.

HAND: Those were the days.

FOOT: The days of walking, running.

HAND: (*Stares for being interrupted*) Perhaps I did hold the wind, the darkness, even the sounds curling through leaves, the blackness whispering from my fingers.

RAGWEED: You stripped the land, made the rocks bleed, gave living streams the drink of death and thirst for more.

HAND: (*Not listening*) Whispering from my fingers, I shaped the earth, darling of my dreams.

RAGWEED: Even I, flying on wind, able to love even stone, choked where my roots went down.

HAND: (*Realizing what Ragweed is saying*) And what difference is it?

FOOT: No place even for me, I who am all motion.

RAGWEED: Are we to know who we are? Or what we do?

HAND: What difference?

FOOT: I am where I am.

HAND: You are where you go.

RAGWEED: Or stay.

HAND If I break glass am I broken glass?

RAGWEED: If you break wind you are broken wind. (*Foot and Ragweed laugh*)

HAND: Be serious.

RAGWEED: Sorry.

HAND: Perhaps we should not talk of before?

FOOT: Since everything is now?

HAND: Yes.

RAGWEED: No. I like to hear of before, even now.

HAND: (*Looking at hands*) Five fingers wide. Is that all? I always thought it more.

FOOT: Why so?

HAND: All they did. All the building, the holding, the touching.

FOOT: The tearing down, the killing.

HAND: Yes, I suppose I must admit that too. I wonder why I never want to admit that?

RAGWEED: The ripping apart the land.

HAND: That too.

FOOT: So there's no place for me to be.

HAND: And even then does it matter? I build. I shape stones and great structures rise into the sky. I tear down, and kill and men die and the stones and men become dust for new stones and men sometime beyond.

FOOT: What are you saying?'

HAND: I'm not sure.

RAGWEED: Say it again.

HAND: I can't remember.

RAGWEED: Talk about before.

FOOT: Will that get us closer to the answer?

HAND: Who knows? When we decided to come here, we only promised to search for the answer, not find it.

RAGWEED: Shall I talk of before?

FOOT: Let Hand finish. There is time for all our turns.

HAND: Shall I begin in spring?

RAGWEED: You've already begun once.

HAND: When time is forever, one can begin as many times as he likes.

FOOT: But he can never end.

RAGWEED: Is that the answer?

HAND: No, a question.

RAGWEED: Before, I want to hear of before.

HAND: First, before I begin again, I want to say something else.

FOOT: Do we have a choice?

RAGWEED: Here we have all choices.

HAND: And no choices.

FOOT: Even if we can't decide, let's decide anyway. Say what you want.

HAND: Are you sure?

RAGWEED: Foot is never sure. Go ahead.

HAND: The tearing down. I've been thinking of the tearing down, and the killing. I don't think it matters. I tear up the land, it is torn land. If the earth tears up the land, if mountains rise screaming in the dawn, if earthquakes shatter the silence, if wind, rain wash all away into the sea until the sea becomes land, it is torn land. If I kill, man dies. If I do not kill, man dies. Whatever, the land is torn. Whatever, man dies.

RAGWEED: Rationalization.

HAND: What?

RAGWEED: Rationalization. You merely rationalize.

HAND: I build.

FOOT: And tear down.

RAGWEED: And rationalize. You come from a nation of rationalization. And guilt. You feel guilty, so you must rationalize.

FOOT: Look. More come. (*Looks at audience*)

HAND: It will be awhile before they can see us.

RAGWEED: Before. Begin again of before.

HAND: I cleared the land, moved back the tree line till there was no line, only land. (*Holding out hands*) These broke the earth, even built the plow before breaking, and held seeds before planting. These held life becoming.

RAGWEED: I was there with none of that. I needed only wind.

HAND: Then these guided, held destiny.

RAGWEED: Rationalization.

FOOT: Now that you are all memory, how would you want to be remembered?

HAND: The builder.

FOOT: But you destroyed more than you built.

HAND: Very well then. Say that I touched, that I came and touched. Say that I found a wilderness and brought it tame till the sorrow grew like swelling pain and I seek the wilderness again.

FOOT: It is gone. There is no return.

RAGWEED: I was always wilderness, and you and you who now know, even now fear it so.

FOOT: Whose turn now?

RAGWEED: Since I was first, I will also be last. Go ahead. Foot.

FOOT: I've forgotten the question.

HAND: It's so easy to get lost. I can't remember, but I think it had something to do with worth.

FOOT: Before or now?

HAND: I'm not sure

FOOT: I'll talk of before. Perhaps we'll think of the question.

HAND: Have I already talked of before?

RAGWEED: Yes, I think so. (*Hand moves a short distance from the others and sits down and begins thinking*)

FOOT: First I became uneasy with the land and I searched new land, walked new tracks my own deep down till they grew old and I grew tired and I again searched new land. I have always gone like smoke on the wind—to all corners, even where the angels stood, and beyond.

HAND: You always go.

FOOT: Always. I hear a door open in the wind, with hinges squeaking like dark clouds, and I must go through. Even now there is the door. Even now there is the road, and if no road, a path and if nothing, I begin—knowing others will follow. Did you say worth?

HAND: I can't remember. I think so.

FOOT: Perhaps that is the answer. Nothing is deeper than the shoe.

RAGWEED: Maybe the question.

FOOT: Tracks are immortal.

RAGWEED: You forget the rain. It washes them away.

FOOT: Then I will make new tracks.

RAGWEED: Now? Look where you go down. You leave no mark.

FOOT: (*Turns to look back the way he entered*) You're right, but still I go. Even now, I can go if I choose.

RAGWEED: Talk of before.

FOOT: Before. I don't know where I began –only that I did. I never knew, nor now, where I was going. Even when I stood still, it was my choice. Likewise to go. At first there were not paths and I made them. Then roads. It didn't matter. I could choose to go, although often I did not know why I did. Once I walked on water.

HAND: Captured rain. The tracks were gone before you stood.

FOOT: Once I stood on the moon.

HAND: Reflected sun. Even then the tracks were done.

RAGWEED: This land (*pointing*). Where did you go here?

FOOT: Everywhere. Once this was a new, strange land and my coming was a mystery. Then the tracks grew old. Some you destroyed (*pointing to Hand*). Some the rain washed away. Some I think I only dreamed I made. I came from darkness into light. Now it is darkness again.

HAND: Now you are all dream.

FOOT: Yes, but wherever I can dream, I can go. I've still that choice.

HAND: But only I can build a dream.

FOOT: Or tear one down.

RAGWEED: Is there no more before for you except your going?

FOOT: Deciding to go.

RAGWEED: Is it my turn?

FOOT: I can't remember.

RAGWEED: Then it doesn't matter. It will be my turn. I will talk of before.

HAND: How can you, Ragweed? You are neither memory nor dream.

FOOT: And you have no choice.

HAND: And you cannot build.

FOOT: Nor tear down.

RAGWEED: True. You can touch and you and they remember your touch. And you can choose to go, and go. Your touch fades with memory, and your tracks die in dreams. I am always.

HAND: Yet, you are worthless.

RAGWEED: I do not have to decide. If there is wind, I go. If there is none, I fall there, death wrapped around my shell, but life bursts out and I grow and wait for new winds to blow. Even in death, I am alive.

HAND: The answer, my friend, is blowing on the wind.

FOOT: What?

HAND: I'm not sure. I think it's from memory.

FOOT: Tell me again. Perhaps it's from dream.

HAND: I can't remember.

RAGWEED: I have no need for dream nor memory. I need only my lover wind.

HAND: And if there is no wind?

RAGWEED: Then I have not need.

HAND: If you have no memory, how can you talk of before?

RAGWEED: I am always.

HAND: Is that enough?

RAGWEED: It is all.

HAND: Still, is that enough?

FOOT: Look. More come. Without sound, they slip from there to here.

HAND: Perhaps they will know the answer.

FOOT: Or the question.

RAGWEED: And there. The clouds announce the first sun.

HAND: And the night's end.

FOOT: Should we greet them?

HAND: They cannot see us yet.

FOOT: Then we must follow the night?

HAND: Always.

RAGWEED: The sun will find me, burst away the shell.

FOOT: Will we meet here again?

HAND: Yes. By chance or choice.

RAGWEED: One question. If the land could speak, which of us
            would it choose?

HAND: It chose all of us.

*(They begin walking around as if futilely attempting to greet the
new ones, then exit very slowly back stage. The song "Ragweed"
begins almost immediately after the last speech)*

Ragweed

(Chorus and first stanza)
The sun shaves the frost
From the cold, cold ground.
The hair of the blue wind fall.
Come this time another year around
And I won't be here at all.

Lee Pennington

The size of the hand
Is five fingers wide,
The foot as deep as the shoe.
Stars burn on a cold, winter night;
So tell me why don't you.

Chorus.

Ragweed grows in yonder field;
He grows so green and tall
Spreads his seeds everywhere,
Anywhere they will fall.

Chorus.

(Curtain)

TIMBER AGAIN

Lee Pennington

Back on the Land   *by Jill Baker*

FORGOTTEN STUMPS

I have forgotten time and days
no longer have numbers. Only May,
the month of May, and even that
grows unsure. What time she asks
and I say the time of moon
blowing clouds behind trees.
It is the time of river
and wild ducks mating of spring.
Time of giant laurel and long
black strangers making dead
leaf sounds and old chestnut
stumps, the last grey love ghosts
something being born in earth again.

Lee Pennington

BACK ON THE LAND

I am back on the land
my father's land
and his father's land
and before them just land.

And I stand
surefooted in the deep black soil
where men greater than I stood singing
of mules and of corn, and of struggle.

Yet they wrote no lines, these poets
none save rows of corn poor
green plants in crabgrass pushing
up through stones of the past.

Wild gooseneck hoes and turning plows
tearing love from the newground wilderness
and pale women with sudden sunbursts
burning flush red into their faces
wiping back a stream of blond hair from eyes
staring deeply into the land.

And a child blanket rolled
in the shade of giant white oaks standing
like guards at the end of the field.

This was their land made by calloused hands
made by bleeding sounds and weeping
and near still laughter
and a handful of pride strong
as steel and I weak and silly
from too much town
am their poetry their child their line
written on a hillside page
my father's land
his father's land
and before them just land.

Lee Pennington

THE OLD WORLD

The old world limps toward now.
Along the gravel road back farther
than yesterday caught green.
Old world full of broken men
and breaking women.
The fire drips ashes earthward.
Like spring never come.
Like the no sky rain.
The no tree wind.
For this the solid rumble
for now the never.
The old world caught wanting
dragging its feet toward the new.

IN THE MOUNTAINS

Give me your broken and lonely
where skies are grey ice above.
Let me hear people again singing
even if they don't know love.

Let me see their dark stained faces
know their feet bruised to blood.
If all the rains stop falling,
let the streams be loaded with mud.

Give me that last song's tune
the lonely unwilling to cry
and if I hear strange singing
let me not pass it by.

ATAVISM

"He will return like beavers to the Rhone,"
I heard uncle say. Together faces wind blown

we watched sand-like pollen fly from the hay.
I was eight then had muscles like creek clay

thoughts like frog eggs in the branch bed
all rolled up in me like a storm-coming thunderhead.

But I could not believe he would return, rebuild;
I saw too many sprouts in the unplowed field.

If he were near he couldn't stand that.
He would be out at dawn laying sprouts flat.

But uncle was a smart man, school teacher well read.
So I listened carefully-heard all that he said.

"Yes, he will come when those sprouts turn to timber.
He'll come sneaking back in like the month of December!'

I wondered what uncle meant, "beavers on the River
          Rhone,"
big knotty hand scholar-red face, sharp bone.

Today uncle rests near Dad in the clay;
my son swings a hatchet at sprouts in his way.

SUCH A DISTANCE

It was hard to tell
at such a distance
if there were one or three—
a man a mule a plow
against the hill
in perfect symmetry.

And farther back
greater distance still
even the land with subtle glance
became one with three
and only widening furrows
changed that symmetry.

I had been closer years
gone by and knew surely each—
man mule, plow and land—
when I first heard some voice speak:
"We are one not what you see."
But I did not understand.

It takes a distance
to see close up land;
it takes a space to know.
Now I've been to earth
and back again
with no place else to go.

CANEY MOUNTAIN

We stood atop Caney Mountain
where the wind had left grey this sea
turned sky of boulders. High above
the last falling water we tumbled through
leaves piled several winters deep and found
ourselves drifting in fallen seasons.
Over the edge of space we first knew the earth
for here we could see it all
spread out before us like weeds at dawn
covered with spider webs blue as shadows.

LIGHT WEIGHT

He set about to weigh the light
lifting hands sky up to spread the sun
fall, and guessed it little more than whispers
less than feathers perhaps the same as dreams.
Even so, how to measure, what to use as balance—
both heavier. Still he would try laying
guess on guess till he somehow got it right.
And at last in the final dawn greying,
knew it would be enough to break the night.

Lee Pennington

SHADOWS OF VIOLETS

This morning in the hush of dawn
I go into the dark woods
under tall oaks
this before the sun spills over.
To the east it is grey
and to the west still dark
the chill feeling black of the last traces
of night hanging on.
It is April and odors say it such.

I wait.
First the hush broken by song
a redbird flutters
in the low bushes ahead
and a wind ever so slight
brings crackly sounds of limbs rubbing together.
A leaf falls from above me;
it is fresh from winter victory.
Now spring shoves it away
frees it back to earth.
The wind plays with it
turns it this way and that
teases it sometimes
then passes on to leave it, forever.

Down by the trunks of the oaks
where moss makes a nest
purple violets push up through dark soil

lie fresh in the twilight.
And maybe I think a thousand autumns
have laid cover of leaves
and blankets of rain have
turned them back to earth again.
Now the soil is dark and the loam rich
and here lush purple violets
and tiny babytears can grow.

When the sun rises touching first
the tree tops and later lower
pale shadows fall beyond the flowers
and I watch a new wind
delicate and frail
play with the colors
the tiny blues and purples
and their grey shadows dance
softly in the light.

I think of the last years
the many leaves fallen
the many times I have wept
I am man and crying.
I think of our age unweeping
and I weep.
I think of people
their tiny purple heads
rising up from dark leaf made loam
and I am one with my shadow
which falls before me.

Lee Pennington

Still the leaves fall.
I have seen them fight the winter with love
and die with the spring.
Still I weep perhaps because of.

They are the top soil of our minds.
Now they soak the rains
cup gentle water till we look down and see
our faces in wet mirrors.

Shall I name the leaves?
I know them all for they are part of me
part of every person
who walks by his shadow on the dark earth
I part of every person
every person part of me.

I wept yesterday
I weep today
I will weep tomorrow.

The leaves have fallen.
Somewhere in the night
each sun gone down
whisper voices tug at roots
of our being.
We ask what can we do?

Let us at least be violets.

ANCIENT RIVER NEW

The river lays flat, brown, still—
the color of dried eyes.
Bumblebees work blooming weeds
wake them to wind motion without wind.
Blackbirds talk about it
as if the day like they
needs disturbed.
Old roots lie piled on the sides—
too wet a spring
too dry a summer.

I have come here moved naturally
as the sycamores white peeling
or willows fighting green to year another ring.

Wild machines crawl on the white bridge
growl for space above the dead water.

I have come naturally
feeling something new as white violets
yet no less ancient than millions
of sea animals frozen in stone
stared beyond dreams a shadow maze
knowing full well with each week's beginning
we are running out of Sundays.

Lee Pennington

MILKWOOD

I sometimes walk when milkwood is in season
and later go where fish grey blooms
burst hair covered seeds to flying then reason
frail white on broken wind zooms
upward till air is mostly sailing things.
I am awed with such immortality
that lush wild juice milkwood brings
swinging and swaying them free—
the earth promising their stay
the wind pushing them away.

ground*

SPRING THAWS

Spring thaws brought deep ruts
under heavy traffic
and roadways, feet and tires
set nearly immobile, left us
clawing to free ourselves.
It is a clinging thing
this rebirth this spring
unlike frozen winter
and dried summer
when we move swiftly surely.
Now there is pain coming
total from prison mud
dripping and slinging our feet
and dancing ourselves
clean in the grass.

167

Lee Pennington

TO THE SOIL

I relish your praise
(for I am a man and men do)
and I spread my arms
till they are broad enough
to hold both praise and you.

I love soft whispers
that sink like dew
into my cornstalk blades
and spider roots
and I go wise at the way
you sing of the singer.

But wise also of other things
other times and darker woods
where I first grew
even as I taste the sweetness
of loving you
I must also (for still I am a man)
be true.

I must say
wings you make of me
are neither the bird nor I
and even with all my flapping
I cannot fly.

RETURN

I return again; but it is not much, not here
where earth once more is green and fields
are gone where all is scars of sunlight,
a purple stone face some night artist builds
of the last long streaks falling west.
It is not much for now sprouts are timber
and the tall rows of corn in a plowed
newground earth are about all I can remember
of the time you stood by the spider roots
spoke of the land and sky spoke of needs
for one schooled in fighting a stone loved hill
yet never a single victory with the weeds.
But know this, my father, with the world in stress
I battle now not against but with the wilderness.

Lee Pennington

FINALLY

If I return to the land to stay
(and as a last resort I will)
what shall be my gift
other than myself
and what shall be its gift
other than itself?

We give each other each other
a kind of court house square
horse trade
where I say,

"Now look, land,
I don't mind this gift"
(You'll get me anyway)
"I just want a little room—
six feet soon long and deep
and a yard wide
and that will be enough."

And it says,

"Fine, so long as
you don't turn on me."

Then we trade
dropping our knives
each with a broken blade.

Baby Tears (Bleeding Heart)   *by Jill Baker*

www.ingramcontent.com/pod-product-compliance
Lightning Source LLC
Chambersburg PA
CBHW030929090426
42737CB00007B/367